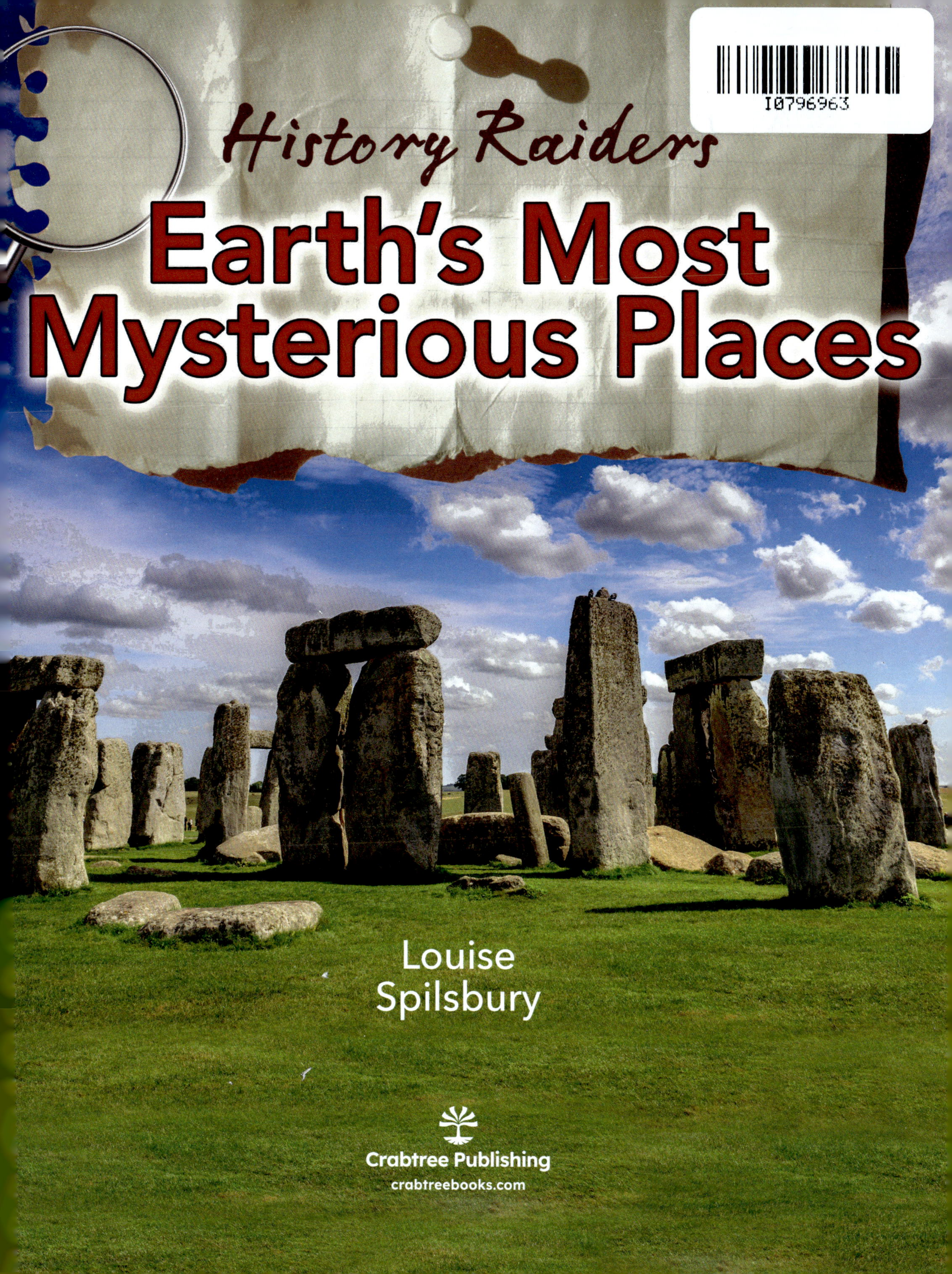

History Raiders

Earth's Most Mysterious Places

Louise Spilsbury

Crabtree Publishing
crabtreebooks.com

Crabtree Publishing

crabtreebooks.com 800-387-7650

In Canada: We acknowledge the financial support of the Government of Canada through the Canada Book Fund for our publishing activities.

Published in Canada
Crabtree Publishing
616 Welland Avenue
St. Catharines, Ontario
L2M 5V6

Published in the United States
Crabtree Publishing
347 Fifth Avenue
Suite 1402-145
New York, NY 10016

Author: Louise Spilsbury
Editors: Sarah Eason, Jennifer Sanderson, and Janine Deschenes
Proofreader and indexer: Tracey Kelly
Proofreader: Crystal Sikkens
Editorial director: Kathy Middleton
Design: Jessica Moon
Cover design: Katherine Berti
Photo research: Rachel Blount
Prepress and print coordination: Katherine Berti
Consultant: Rupert Matthews

Written, developed, and produced by Calcium

Printed in Canada/052024/CPC20240514

Library and Archives Canada Cataloguing in Publication
Title: Earth's most mysterious places / Louise Spilsbury.
Names: Spilsbury, Louise, author.
Description: Series statement: History raiders | Includes bibliographical references and index.
Identifiers: Canadiana (print) 20210192534 | Canadiana (ebook) 20210192542 | ISBN 9781427151032 (hardcover) | ISBN 9781427151094 (softcover) | ISBN 9781427151155 (HTML) | ISBN 9781427151216 (EPUB)
Subjects: LCSH: Curiosities and wonders—Juvenile literature.
Classification: LCC AG244 .S65 2022 | DDC j001.94—dc23

Photo Credits: t=Top, c=Center, b=Bottom, l= Left, r=Right

Cover: Shutterstock; Inside: Shutterstock: Alexander P: p. 16 cl; Anton Ivanov: p. 25; Kyle Cr8on: p. 8 cl; Danyssphoto: p. 19; Digital Storm: pp. 3 & throughout; Garykingphotographer: p. 11; Grafvision: p. 20 tl; Nicholas Grey: p. 21; Stefano Guidi: p. 10; Tero Hakala: p. 22; Hitforsa: p. 7; Jeanrenaud Photography: p. 18; Gregorio Koji: p. 23; Willem Kruger: p. 12 tl; Henning Marquardt:p. 27; Miriam Park: pp. 13, 29 bl; Snapper Nick: p. 24 tl; Vorobiov Oleksii 8: p. 24 cl; Photo Junction: p. 8 tl; Simon Pittet: p. 14; Regissercom: p. 15; Reimar: pp. 16 tl, 17; Natalia Sedyakina: p. 12 cl; Standret: pp. 16, 29 tr; Stockshoppe: p. 20 cl; WindVector: p. 6; Wikimedia Commons: Lt. Comdr. Horace Bristol, U.S. Navy: pp. 9, 28; Mario Modesto Mata: p. 26; Mpmajewski: p. 5; NASA: p. 4.

Hardcover 978-1-4271-5103-2
Paperback 978-1-4271-5109-4
Ebook (pdf) 978-1-4271-5115-5
Epub 978-1-4271-5121-6

Library of Congress Cataloging-in-Publication Data
Names: Spilsbury, Louise, author.
Title: Earth's most mysterious places / Louise Spilsbury.
Description: New York, NY : Crabtree Publishing Company, [2022] | Series: History raiders | Includes index.
Identifiers: LCCN 2021016394 (print) | LCCN 2021016395 (ebook) | ISBN 9781427151032 (hardcover) | ISBN 9781427151094 (paperback) | ISBN 9781427151155 (ebook) | ISBN 9781427151216 (epub)
Subjects: LCSH: Curiosities and wonders--Juvenile literature. | History--Miscellanea--Juvenile literature. | Geography--Miscellanea--Juvenile literature.
Classification: LCC AG244 .S65 2022 (print) | LCC AG244 (ebook) | DDC 031.02--dc23
LC record available at https://lccn.loc.gov/2021016394
LC ebook record available at https://lccn.loc.gov/2021016395

CONTENTS

MYSTERIOUS EARTH

Many places around the world are cloaked in mystery. These places are strange, sometimes spooky, and even bizarre. Over the centuries, people have struggled to explain how they came to be. The strange occurrences or things found there are often even harder to explain.

Stories and Mystery

One such mysterious place is in the Sahara in Africa. A gigantic rock swirl called the Richat Structure is found there. Viewed from space, the 30-mile (48.2 km) swirl looks like a giant snail shell or a staring eye. Some people think it could be the landing site of an alien spaceship. It could also be the **remains** of an ancient building. Others say it is an unusual **meteoric crater**.

Strange Flames

The Eternal Flame Falls in a **remote** part of New York's Chestnut Ridge Park is a stunning waterfall with a strange secret. Behind the cascades of flowing water glows a strange orange-red light. There is a small fire at the core of the falls that burns day and night. According to local **legends**, a Native American lit the flame long ago, and it has burned ever since—but no one is certain what really causes this curious **phenomenon**.

The Richat Structure is also known as the Eye of the Sahara.

One theory about Eternal Flame Falls is that gas seeps through a hole in the rock below the waterfall, and this gas burns, causing the flames.

Explore History

In this book, we will journey across the world to discover the stories behind the most mysterious places. As we do so, we will examine questions raised by these strange places and gather **evidence** to try and answer them.

History Raider!

Hey! I'm Madison Maverick. I'm an explorer. I also like to think of myself as a history raider—a person who stops at nothing to find answers about the past. Come with me on my journeys to solve past mysteries and answer questions about history. Read my field notes on the History Raider pages and boxes. Then, jot down evidence to help solve each mystery.

THE BERMUDA TRIANGLE

The Bermuda Triangle is a triangular-shaped stretch of sea off the North Atlantic Ocean. It sits between Bermuda, Florida, and the Greater Antilles Islands, which include Puerto Rico and Cuba. Stories of lost sailors, disappearing ships, and crashed aircraft have haunted the Bermuda Triangle for years.

Dangerous Waters

In 1492, the famous explorer Christopher Columbus first sailed in the area. He spotted strange lights in the sky. Since then, there have been reports of unexplained disappearances in the Bermuda Triangle. Over the years, more than 20 planes and 50 ships have been known to crash or disappear completely in the area. Many people believe hundreds or even thousands more planes and ships have fallen victim to the Bermuda Triangle's strange powers.

Lost at Sea

One lost ship was the USS *Cyclops*. It left Barbados in March 1918 and disappeared with all 309 people on board. Neither the wreck nor any survivors have ever been found. One of the most mysterious disappearances happened in 1945. On December 5, five bomber planes disappeared during a routine training flight known as Flight 19. The bombers were never seen again.

The Bermuda Triangle covers around 500,000 square miles (1,294,994 km^2) of water.

Scary Secrets?

Many people believe that these events have no obvious or logical explanation. The legend of the Bermuda Triangle puts off many travelers from passing directly through this area of ocean. Some are scared by stories of giant and terrifying sea monsters. Others fear that space portals, or holes, in the sea may open up and swallow ships. Some people think there may even be **supernatural** forces at work.

Freak waves and sudden storms have been known to sink ships without warning. Is this the answer to the Bermuda Triangle mystery?

History Raider!

As soon as I learned about the disappearance of Flight 19 in the Bermuda Triangle, I knew I had to investigate. Had mysterious forces caused Flight 19 to disappear, or was there an explanation? Let's investigate!

As my plane came closer to the edge of the area known as the Bermuda Triangle, my hands started to shake. Even though I didn't really believe the stories, the waters below looked dark, deep, and threatening. I started to feel nervous. I kept checking the plane's control panel to see that everything was okay.

Mysterious Reports

I flew onto the base from which the planes in Flight 19 had left. The reports about that fateful day were gloomy. The five doomed planes had set off on a clear, dry afternoon. Four hours later, they disappeared from the sky. A naval air search and rescue plane was sent out to find them. But it vanished, too! Hundreds of search boats were sent out. None of these found any signs of wreckage from the missing planes.

Vanished!

The records showed that while the pilots were still in radio contact with the base, they had reported some problems. One pilot was convinced that his **compass** wasn't working. He believed that the planes were flying in the wrong direction. The pilots also reported entering an area of heavy clouds, wind, and rain. One was heard to say, "I don't know where we are... We're completely lost..." Then, suddenly, the radio went dead.

The planes that set out that day in 1945 for a routine training flight over the Bermuda Triangle were doomed never to return.

What Happened?

I did some research into the search and rescue aircraft that disappeared. I discovered that a passing ship had seen a **fireball** that day and found an oil slick in the ocean. This could be evidence that the rescue plane exploded shortly after takeoff. But what about the five planes that were part of Flight 19? Reports showed that the pilots were very confused about their location. Perhaps the planes were lost for so long that they ran out of fuel and plunged into the ocean. In that case, it is likely that the pilots drowned in the rough seas and deep water.

Finding Answers

That was a pretty mysterious case! Did you find evidence from my field notes that might explain the disappearance? Turn to pages 28–29 to discover if your findings match mine.

MYSTERIOUS PATTERNS

Reports of strange geometric patterns suddenly appearing in fields have sparked curiosity around the world. These patterns are called crop circles. One early set of crop circles appeared in Tully, Australia, in 1966. A farmer there found a roughly circular area of flattened grass in a field. He thought it had been made by a flying saucer. Many people who study crop circles believe they could be messages from intelligent alien beings.

Crop Circles

From the late 1970s to the 1990s, crop circles appeared overnight in grassy fields throughout the United Kingdom (U.K.). Some were simple circles, but others were incredibly complex **geometric** patterns. Some people suggested they were made by unusual wind patterns. Others thought undetectable **energy fields** created them. However, in 1991, two men confessed that they made some of the patterns. They did it as a stunt after reading about the circles in Australia. However, they also said that they did not make all of the circles. No one has come forward to confess to making the others.

Some people believe that crop circles like these found in Turin, Italy, were made by unidentified flying objects (UFOs).

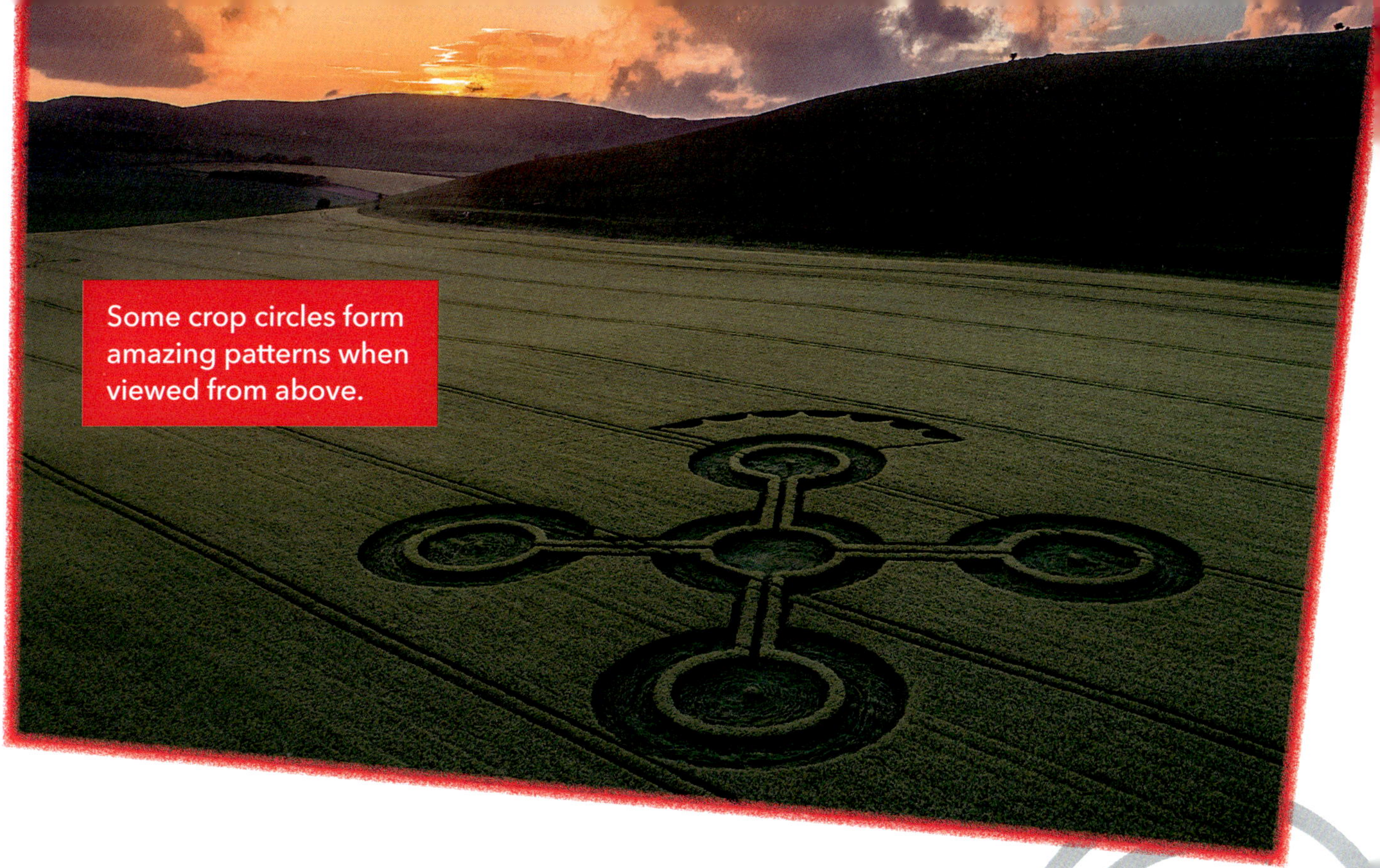

Some crop circles form amazing patterns when viewed from above.

The Fairy Circles of Namibia

Some of the strangest crop circles in the world are in Namibia, in southwest Africa. In desert grasslands, there are spaces 20 feet (6 m) long where no plants grow. These mysterious circles range from 7 feet (2 m) to 49 feet (15 m) in **diameter**. The circles have grown and shrunk over a period of 30 to 60 years. In Namibia, local legends call them "fairy circles." Some say they are footprints of ancient gods who gave the circles magical powers.

History Raider!

The fairy circles of Namibia are intriguing. Could the formation of these perfectly round spaces of short grass be down to magical powers, or is there another explanation? Time to find out...

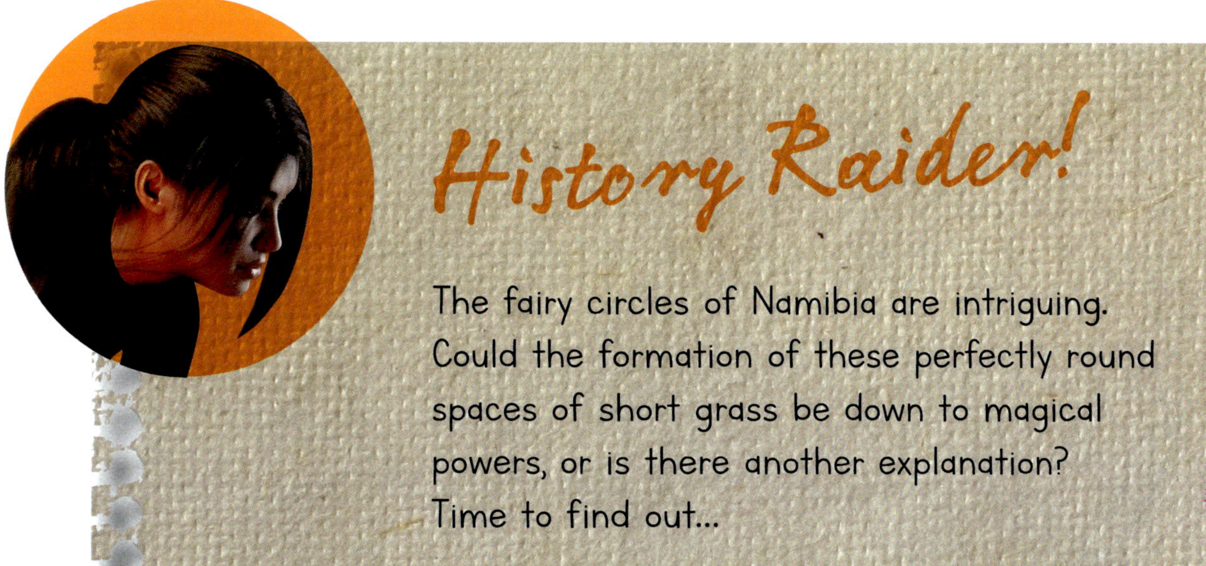

History Raider!

Secrets in the Sand

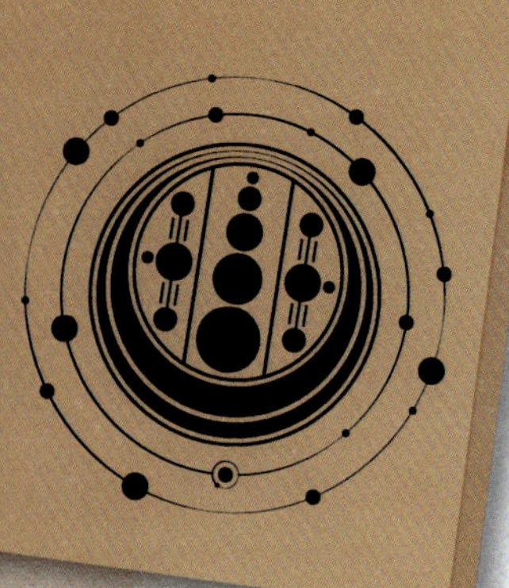

By the time I landed in the dusty Namib desert in Namibia, my head was full of the strange stories told to explain the fairy circles. My favorite was a local tale of dragons that live underground. The legend says that the dragons breathe poison that kills the plants, causing the bare areas of desert. I was convinced I could find the real answer to this mystery through science.

Insect Attack?

The first thing that I spotted as I walked among the spooky circles were a few termites scurrying about in the sand. I know that termites live in large groups called colonies, and that these bugs live most of their lives underground. The colonies create long tunnels in the soil for the termites to travel underground in. These insects have large, strong jaws that they can use to chomp into and eat the roots of desert grasses buried underground. Could they be the culprits?

It made sense that wherever they set up home, there would be a lot of grass roots eaten. It seemed to me that the dead areas of grass would occur where termites ate all the roots of desert grass in an area. Perhaps the edges of the circular shapes happened because that's where the colony stopped eating.

Greedy Grasses?

Just when I thought I had figured out the mystery, I remembered reading of similar circles in Australia where there were no termites. There must be another explanation for the circles, then. I felt so hot and thirsty in the dry, dusty heat that another thought struck me. Plants growing in this hot desert must have to compete for limited amounts of water to survive. As grass plants in one spot grow larger, their roots get longer and spread underground, gathering precious drops of water from a wider area. This would make it harder for other grass plants to grow in the area without water. New grasses are also more likely to grow where larger grasses are already established, because soil is moister there. Perhaps this was the truth behind the mysterious circles?

What is the real explanation for the mystical fairy circles that appear in Namibia?

Finding Answers

So, what is the truth behind the circles in the Namib desert? The evidence I noted might help uncover it. What did you record? Turn to pages 28–29 to learn if your findings match mine.

CITIES LOST IN TIME

There have been several lost cities in history. Many were said to have suddenly vanished without a trace. Some, such as El Dorado in Colombia, South America, exist only in stories. However, others may have been real.

The City of Gold

El Dorado was described as a city full of treasures of solid gold. It was hidden in the South American jungle. Some people say that the legend of El Dorado came from a true story of sunken treasure in Lake Guatavita in Colombia. There, local people dropped gold and other treasures into the water as offerings to their goddess of water. However, the city of El Dorado has never been found.

Another source of the El Dorado legend comes from the story of a ruler so rich that he covered himself in gold each morning. Then, in the evening, he washed off the gold into the sacred Lake Guatavita.

The Lost City

Atlantis is a legendary city that believers claim was swallowed by the sea in ancient Greek times. The Greek **philosopher** Plato wrote a story about an island that contained gold, silver, and other metals. The island disappeared when earthquakes and floods destroyed it. The story so captured people's imaginations that adventurers and scientists have all tried to find Atlantis. So far, they have all failed!

Atlantis was said to be such a rich island because the powerful princes who lived there conquered many of the lands of the Mediterranean.

The Legend of Troy

The legendary city of Troy was the site of the Trojan War, which was fought between the cities of Troy and Greek Sparta in around the1300s B.C.E. The war was said to have started when Prince Paris of Troy kidnapped Helen, the wife of the king of Sparta. Greek soldiers tricked the Trojans by hiding inside a huge wooden horse, called the Trojan Horse. When the Trojans took the wooden horse inside the city, the Greeks leaped out of it and defeated Troy.

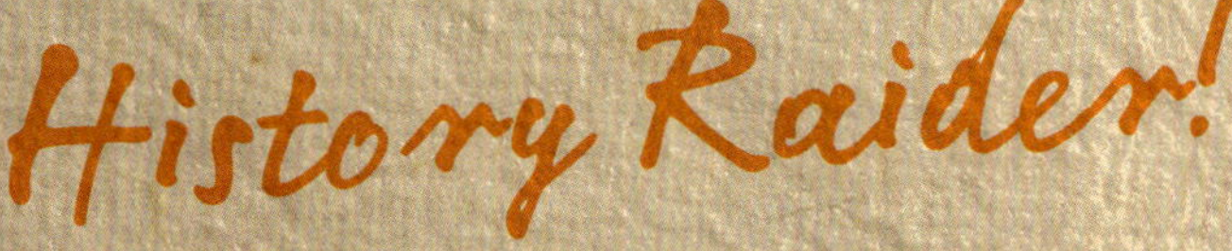

I was so excited by the story of Troy. Some **archaeologists** claim they have found it. Is this true, and what evidence is there to prove their claims? It's time to find out!

History Raider!

Searching for Troy

I felt my heart racing as my plane set down in a hot and dusty region in northwest Turkey. Since ancient times, people have believed that the lost city of Troy was in this area. Would I be able to find it?

Cities beneath the Earth

The rough location of Troy was known about from ancient Greek texts, but the exact site of the city was a secret for thousands of years. In the late 1800s, a German archaeologist named Heinrich Schliemann began to investigate a large **mound** known as Hisarlik. Hisarlik rose 105 feet (32 m) above the ground. This mound was filled with layers of debris from ancient ruined cities. Over time, teams of archaeologists have dug deeper down and discovered nine layers, representing nine different periods of time in which cities were built, lived in, and later destroyed, usually by fire, earthquakes, or both. After one city was destroyed, the survivors simply flattened it out and built a new city on top of it, rather than cleaning up the wreckage.

Could these remains of city walls belong to the ruins of the ancient city of Troy?

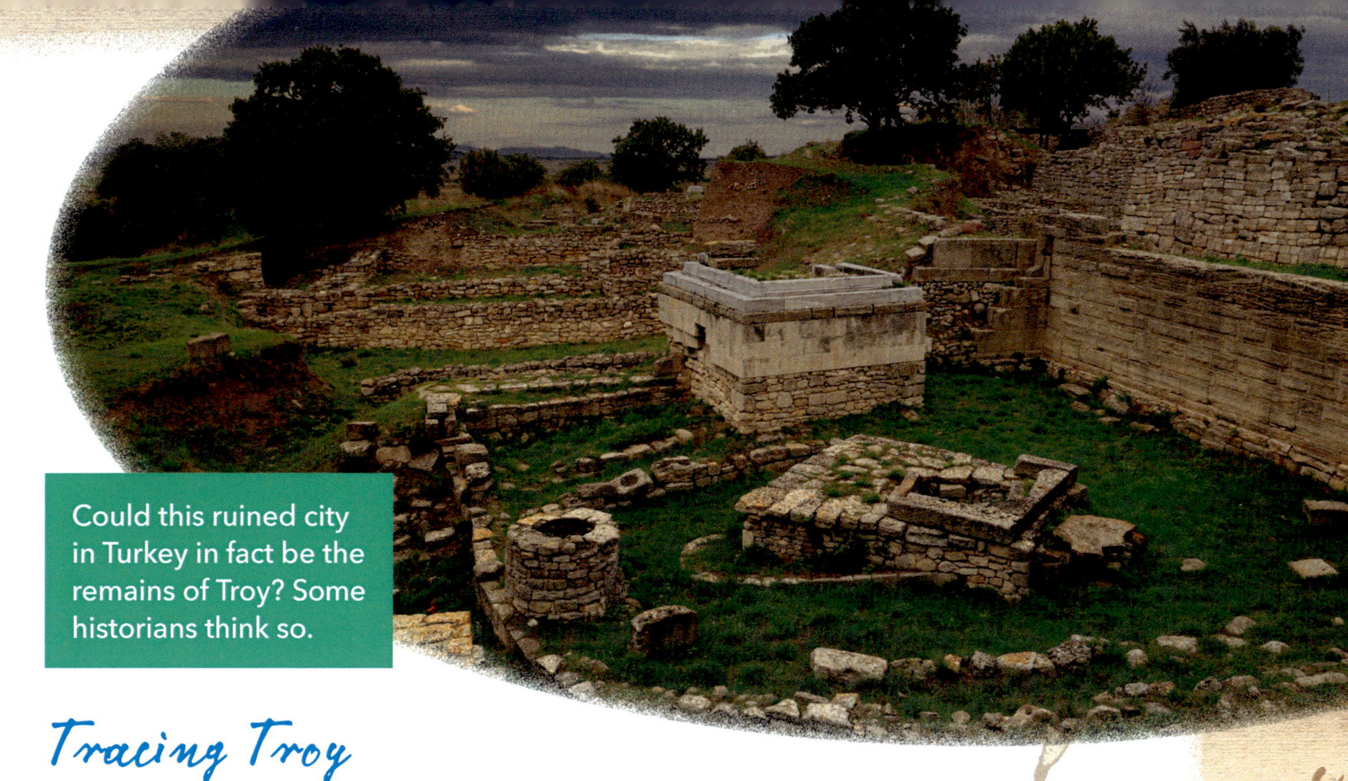

Could this ruined city in Turkey in fact be the remains of Troy? Some historians think so.

Tracing Troy

It was time to study the evidence found in the cities. I discovered that the sixth city, counting from the bottom up in the pile, dates from around 1700 to 1250 B.C.E. This is when the battle of Troy is said to have happened! This city also showed clear signs of being a battle-worn settlement. For example, the ruins of **defensive** walls built around this city show that the people here lived in dangerous times. They expected war. There were also trenches. These were built to store **chariots** that could be ridden into battle. Some of the remains even show signs of an attack from an enemy, with stones scarred by a powerful fire.

Finding Answers

That was an awesome trip! What evidence have you gathered to answer my questions about Troy? Turn to pages 28–29 to learn if your findings match mine.

CIRCLES OF STONE

Thousands of stone circles can be found around the world. A stone circle is a circle or oval of rocks that have been carefully arranged. They were created long ago by ancient peoples. However, no one is certain why they were built or what they were used for.

Sacred Spots

There are different **theories** about how stone circles came to be. Why would ancient people go to the trouble of dragging huge stones long distances and placing them in carefully planned shapes? It is possible that some stone circles were simply places where people met and spent time together. Others are likely to have been places of ceremony and worship. Historians believe some stone circles were built to help people study the movement of the stars and other objects in the sky. They believe this because the stones are lined up with the sun and moon. Perhaps this meant they were used as a type of **prehistoric** calendar.

Drombeg stone circle is a small stone circle in Ireland. It is made up of 17 closely spaced stones.

This is Oianleku, a stone circle in the Basque region of Spain.

Standing Tall

Some stone circles are small. Others are made of giant stones that tower above the landscape and can be seen for miles. Most of these strange constructions are found in Europe, and particularly in the U.K. The most famous is Stonehenge. Found on England's Salisbury Plain in Wiltshire, Stonehenge is a huge circle of standing stones. It was built over many hundreds of years. To this day, there are many theories about who built the circle and why and how they did it. Some people think that the circle was created with the help of the magician Merlin, who features in the stories of **King Arthur**.

History Raider!

Stonehenge has always fascinated me. It is amazing to think that ancient people managed to create this huge circle of stones. It seems to me that they may have needed magic to do it! But is there another explanation? And what was the circle actually used for? Time to find out...

History Raider!

A Sacred Circle

Walking around Stonehenge, I was struck by how significant this impressive site must have seemed to ancient people. Even modern historians and scientists have been baffled by how builders transported the stones. They each weigh up to 24 tons (22 metric tons)—that's the same as four African elephants!

Making the Stone Circle

I looked at the map and realized that the stones could have been dragged on **sleds** to a river or other waterway. They may then have been floated on rafts to move closer to the site. Finally, they could have been hauled out of the water and dragged into position.

Solving the riddle of how they made the circle proved trickier. I saw the remains of stone hammers found near Stonehenge. They gave me a clue as to how the stones were shaped. Hundreds of workers must have spent years shaping and smoothing the stones with these tools. I also found signs of holes in the ground. These could explain how the stones were raised into place. Ancient workers must have dug deep ditches for the base of the stones. They could have used ropes and strong wooden poles and frames to raise them. They probably packed the holes with rocks and rubble to hold them in place.

A Special Place

I took a helicopter trip above the stones to see the circle they form. It was made to line up with the Sun during the summer and winter solstices. Solstices are the longest and shortest days in the year, when the Sun is highest or lowest in the sky at noon. This made me think that Stonehenge was a place where these special days were marked with important ceremonies.

I also found a ring of deep holes around Stonehenge. These may have held a prehistoric fence that once protected it. That made it even more likely that Stonehenge was a kind of temple, or place of worship.

Work at Stonehenge went on for 1,500 years, and took a huge effort from hundreds of well-organized people.

Finding Answers

What evidence have you gathered about why and how ancient people created Stonehenge? Turn to pages 28–29 to learn if your findings match mine.

ISLAND MYSTERY

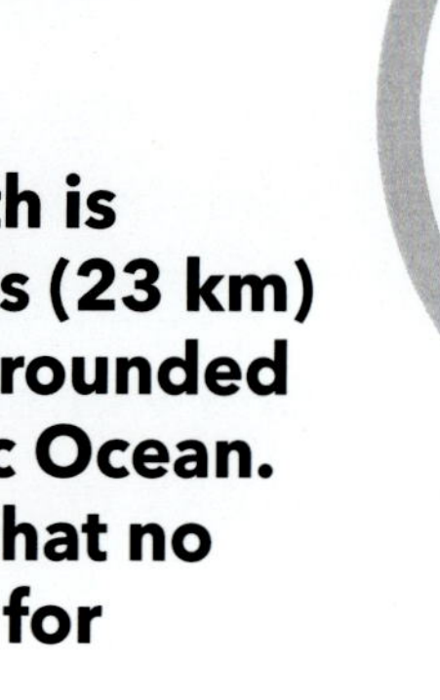

One of the most mysterious islands on Earth is Easter Island. It measures less than 14 miles (23 km) long and just 7 miles (11 km) wide. It is surrounded by almost 2,500 miles (4,023 km) of Pacific Ocean. The island is so far from the coast of Chile that no one other than the islanders knew about it for thousands of years.

Magnificent Moai

In 1722, Dutch explorers stepped off their boats and onto an island with strange giant statues on Easter Sunday. For that reason, they named the island "Easter Island." They were the first outsiders to arrive here. The explorers soon saw the bizarre, giant stone heads dotted all over the land—around 1,000 altogether. Today, these amazing statues, called moai, are known as the Easter Island heads. The moai are up to 40 feet (12 m) tall and weigh up to 88 tons (80 metric tons) each. This is twice the weight of the stones at Stonehenge.

The huge heads that can be seen on land also have full bodies (shown here). The rest of the figures are covered with earth.

Solving a Moai Mystery

Scientists have found that the moai are mainly made from a rock called tuff. Tuff is hardened volcanic ash. It is believed that the tuff on Easter Island was created when a volcano there, named Rano Raraku, erupted long ago. The scientists have also been investigating how the moai were made and positioned all around the island. The islanders have legends with their own explanation. They suggest that the moai were gods who were once able to come to life and walk to their final resting places.

Many of the moai sit upon huge stone platforms or flat mounds known as ahus.

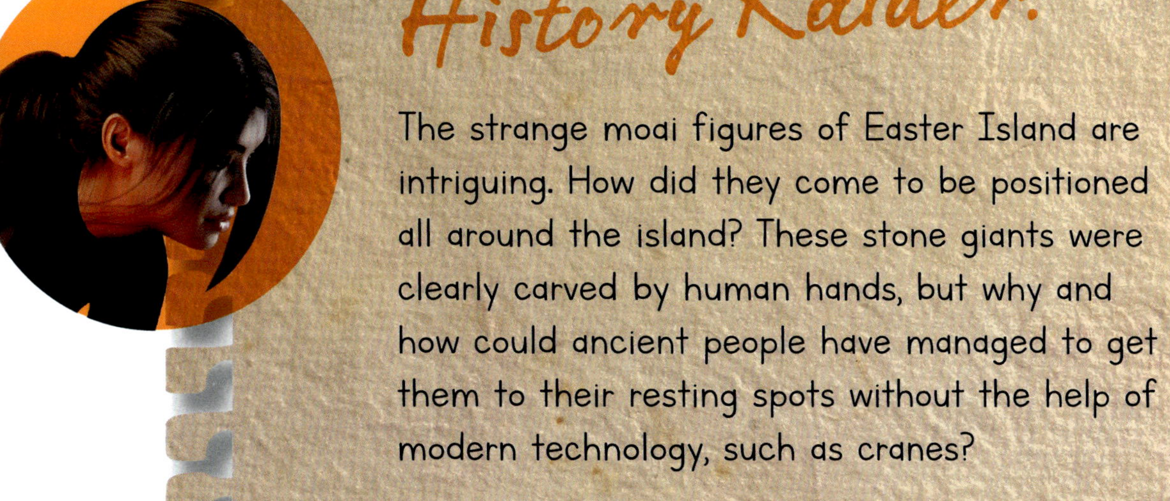

History Raider!

The strange moai figures of Easter Island are intriguing. How did they come to be positioned all around the island? These stone giants were clearly carved by human hands, but why and how could ancient people have managed to get them to their resting spots without the help of modern technology, such as cranes?

As my boat reached the coast of Easter Island, I was awestruck by the strange figures that stood proudly on the land. Were these stone carvings really, as some people believed, gods worshiped by ancient people?

Toki Tools

First, I talked to archaeologists that have studied the moai. They told me that they had discovered tools called toki at Rano Raraku. These stone chisels were made from a very hard kind of rock. It is believed that the chisels were used to carve the moai faces and bodies.

Mystery Solved?

Next, I questioned the archaeologists about how the moai had been placed around the island. Given their size and weight, how could ancient islanders have transported them to their resting places? The archaeologists had some theories. Some said that the stone figures were placed on wooden sleds. Then, they were moved along on rollers to reach their destinations. The rollers could have been made from giant logs. Others say the figures were put on a wooden **rocker** and pulled from side to side. They rocked along the routes to the places where they stood. I wonder if perhaps both methods had been used over time?

Secrets in Their Eyes

I walked across the island to look at more of the statues. As I looked up at a moai, I felt slightly fearful. The faces seemed to be watching me! I also noticed that some of the fearsome-looking characters wore a kind of headdress. That suggested they were powerful and important. Each one was made to look like a real person. Then, I remembered that archaeologists thought the moai statues were built to represent **tribal** chiefs or other important people who had died. As I looked up at the giant statues, I could see how ancient people may have believed the figures were protecting them. Some believed the statues were reminding them to follow the rules of the chiefs.

The word "moai" is a local name for the statues. It translates to "living face of our ancestors."

Finding Answers

Those moai were very mysterious! What evidence did you note about them? Turn to pages 28–29 to learn if your findings match mine.

ONGOING MYSTERIES

New scientific techniques are being invented all the time. In the future, these will help people raid history successfully and answer questions about more of the world's mysterious places.

It's a Date!

Radiocarbon dating is a technique used to find out how old things really are. Most remains contain a substance called carbon, and certain carbon **decays** at the same steady rate. This means that scientists can measure how much of that carbon is left in objects, to figure out how old they are.

Seeing the Invisible

In the future, archaeologists and scientists will discover more about mysterious places using different types of smart technology. For example, they can take pictures of walls using powerful **infrared** lights. These show details that are invisible to the naked eye. For example, they can show images that were once painted on a wall. Though archaeologists in the past had to dig below the ground to find out what was hidden there, in the future, they could use something called ground penetrating **radar** technology. This would allow them to see through the ground without disturbing the surface.

New technology is helping people discover more evidence quickly at archaeological digs.

Looking More Closely

Today, archaeologists are able to use high-powered microscopes to spot traces of substances or signs of wear on objects from the past. This helps them figure out what they were once used for. For example, they can tell if a tool was used for cutting up leather or carving stone figures.

Exploring Hidden Worlds

To explore underwater sites, future robot vehicles will be able to stay underwater for a much longer time. They will be able to produce very detailed maps and images. These robots will also be able to **analyze** what they find deep underwater and report back to researchers on land. In the future, **drones** will be able to fly above remote places and thick jungles—and perhaps discover more mysterious places.

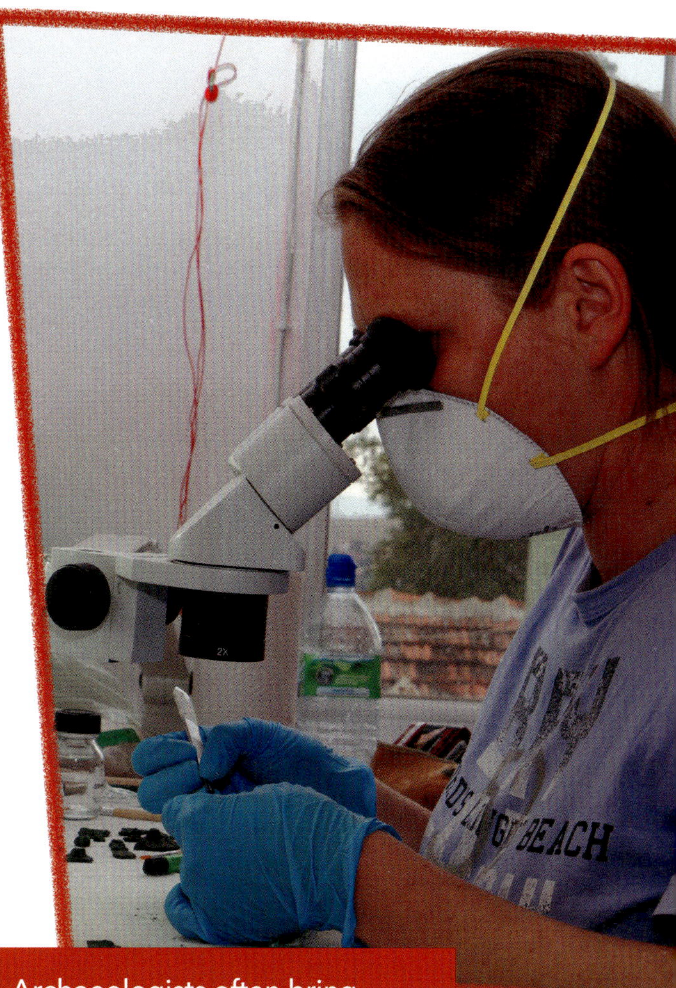

Archaeologists often bring together research on different materials from different sources, such as microscope studies of the chemical makeup of soils. This helps them learn about the history of mysterious places.

History Raider!

For adventurers like us, the world is full of mysteries and wonders to explore. The history of mysterious places has been so much fun to explore, and journeys in the future look just as exciting!

MYSTERY SOLVED?

Some of those places were mysteriously spooky, weren't they? After gathering the evidence, here are some conclusions I made after each journey. How do yours match up?

Pages 8-9: The Case of Flight 19

There's a lot of evidence to suggest that the pilots were lost. One of the pilots was convinced that his compass was not working. He thought they were headed in the wrong direction. A pilot was also heard saying, "We're completely lost ..." before the radio went dead. I think the pilots were lost for so long that they ran out of fuel and crashed into the sea.

Pages 12-13: Secrets in the Sand

I don't believe the circles in Namibia are magical. The dead areas of grass may occur where termites eat all the plant roots there. Perhaps the plants could have grown roots that spread underground to gather water from another area of soil. This would make it harder for plants to grow there, creating the circles.

Pages 16-17: Searching for Troy

The ruined city that archaeologists have found could be Troy. The city dates from around 1700 to 1250 B.C.E., when the Battle of Troy was said to have been fought. The defensive walls link the city to a war. There are also trenches for the chariots used in war.

Pages 20-21: A Sacred Circle

I'm not convinced that magic was used to build Stonehenge. Ancient people could have hauled the rocks on sleds, then taken them some of the way by boat. They could have dug ditches for the base of the stones and used ropes, poles, and frames to raise them. The stones line up with the Sun at the solstices, so they were most likely used for important ceremonies.

Pages 24-25: An Island of Gods

Locals believed that moai walked to their positions. However, there were several theories to explain how they came to be. People could have moved the figures by standing them on sleds and moving them along on rollers. They could have tied them to ropes and rocked them from side to side. The headdresses on some figures suggest they were carved to represent important people.

GLOSSARY

analyze To look at something in detail

archaeologists People who study history through artifacts and remains

chariots Two-wheeled carriages that were pulled by horses and used in battle in ancient times

compass A device for finding direction

decays Rots away

defensive Used to defend or protect

diameter A straight line passing from side to side through the center of a circle

drones Unmanned aircraft

energy fields Regions where energy flows

evidence A sign that shows that something exists or is true

fireball A ball of flame or fire

geometric A pattern of regular shapes

infrared A type of light that feels warm but cannot be seen

King Arthur In stories, a king who lived in England in the Middle Ages

legends Stories from ancient times that are not always true

meteoric crater A bowl-shaped hole made by a rock from space

mound A large pile of something

phenomenon Something that exists and can be seen, especially something unusual

philosopher A person who studies or writes about the meaning of life

prehistoric Before written records

radar A system that uses radio waves to locate objects

remains Pieces or parts of something that are left when most of it has been used up or destroyed

remote Far away from places where people live

rocker A curved bar or similar support on which something can rock

sleds Vehicles on runners that are often pulled by animals and used to transport loads or passengers over snow or ice

supernatural Describes something caused by forces that cannot be explained by science

theories Ideas or thoughts used to explain something

tribal Of a group of people who live together, sharing the same language, culture, and history

LEARNING MORE

BOOKS

Jazynka, Kitson. *History's Mysteries: Curious Clues, Cold Cases, and Puzzles from the Past*. National Geographic Kids, 2017.

Kuligowski, Stephanie. *Unsolved! Mysterious Places* (Time for Kids). Teacher Created Materials, 2012.

Laroche, Giles. *Lost Cities*. HMH Books for Young Readers, 2020.

Stine, Megan. *Where Is the Bermuda Triangle?* Penguin Workshop, 2018.

WEBSITES

Learn more about the Bermuda Triangle at:
https://kids.britannica.com/kids/article/Bermuda-Triangle/598956

See some great pictures and facts about Stonehenge at:
www.natgeokids.com/uk/discover/history/general-history/stonehenge-facts

Read more about Easter Island at:
https://kids.kiddle.co/Easter_Island

Discover more about the Lost City of Atlantis at:
www.natgeokids.com/uk/primary-resource/lost-city-atlantis-primary-resource

INDEX

About the Author

Award-winning author Louise Spilsbury, who also writes under the name Louise Kay Stewart, has written more than 250 books for young people on a wide range of exciting subjects. When not tapping away at the computer keys, she loves swimming in the sea and making bonfires on the beach near her home.